The Triplet Book
for Viola

Part One   by Cassia Harvey

CHP269

©2015 by C. Harvey Publications® All Rights Reserved.

www.charveypublications.com - print books & free sheet music blog
www.learnstrings.com - downloadable books & chamber music

1

Left-Hand Warm-Up: G Major

Cassia Harvey

2

A Sprightly Jig — Trad., arr. Harvey

Paddy the Piper — Trad., arr. Harvey

3

String Crossing

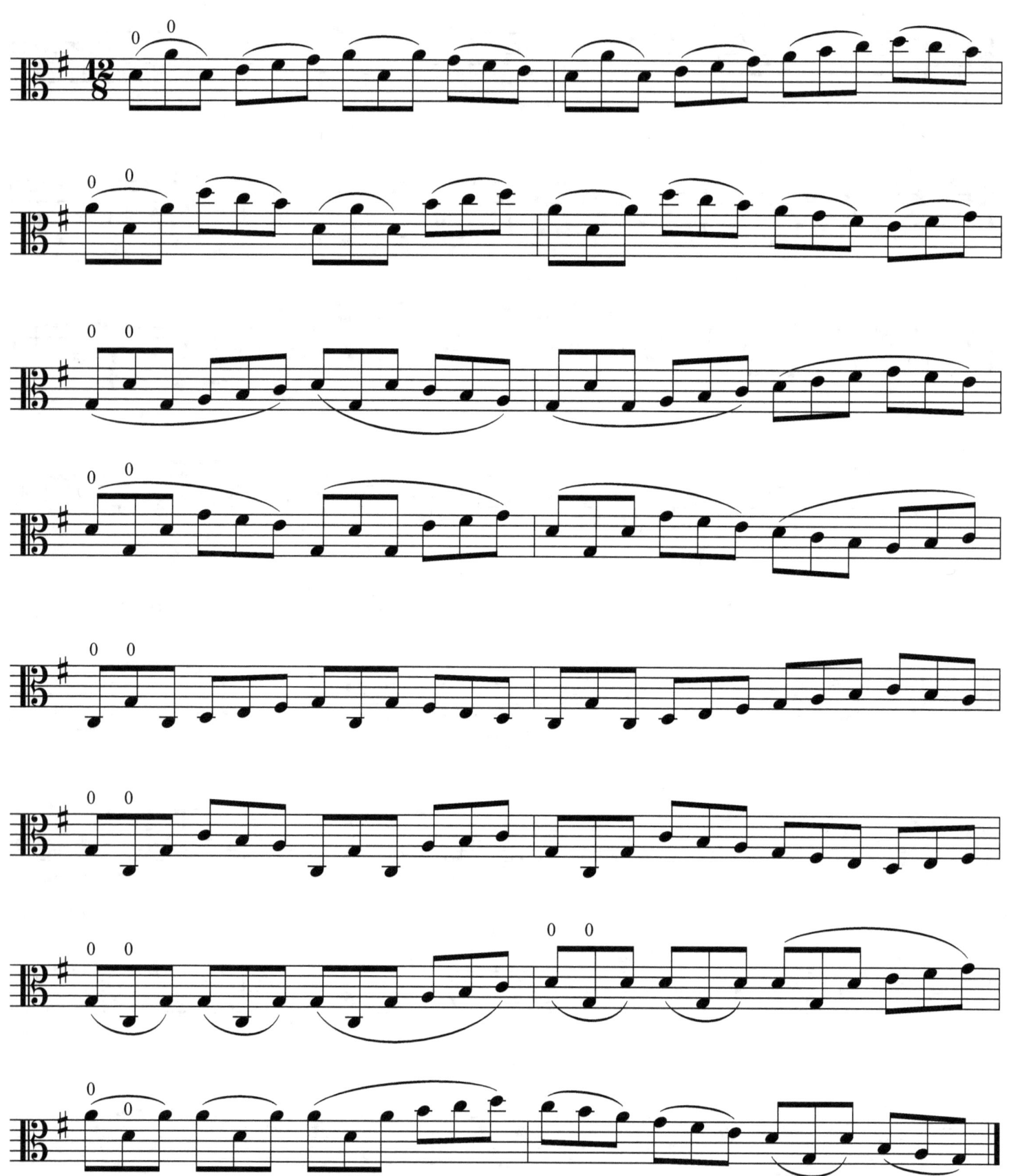

4

The Howlet and the Weazle — Trad., arr. Harvey

Neapolitan Threshers — Trad., arr. Harvey

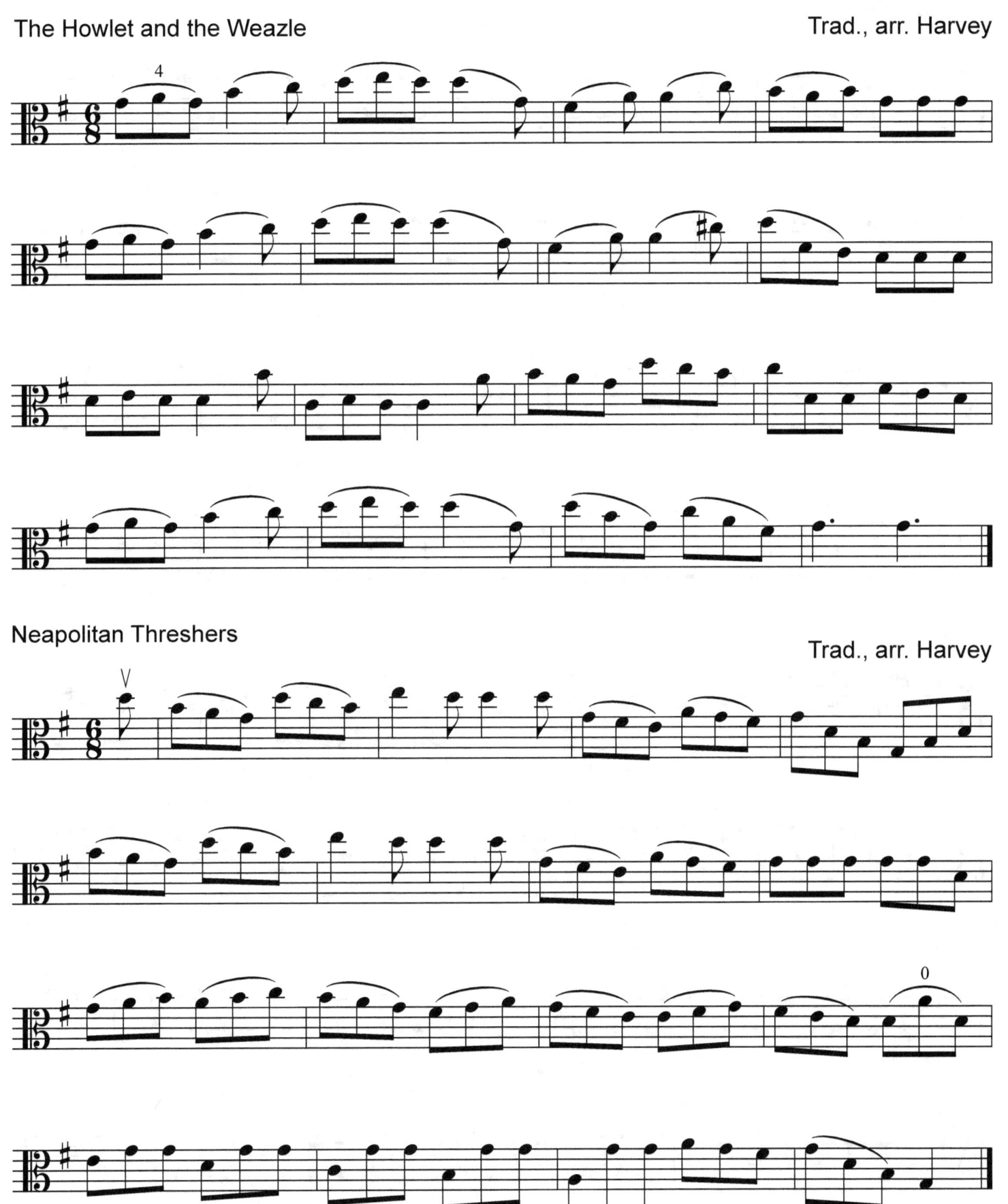

5

Left-Hand Warm-Up

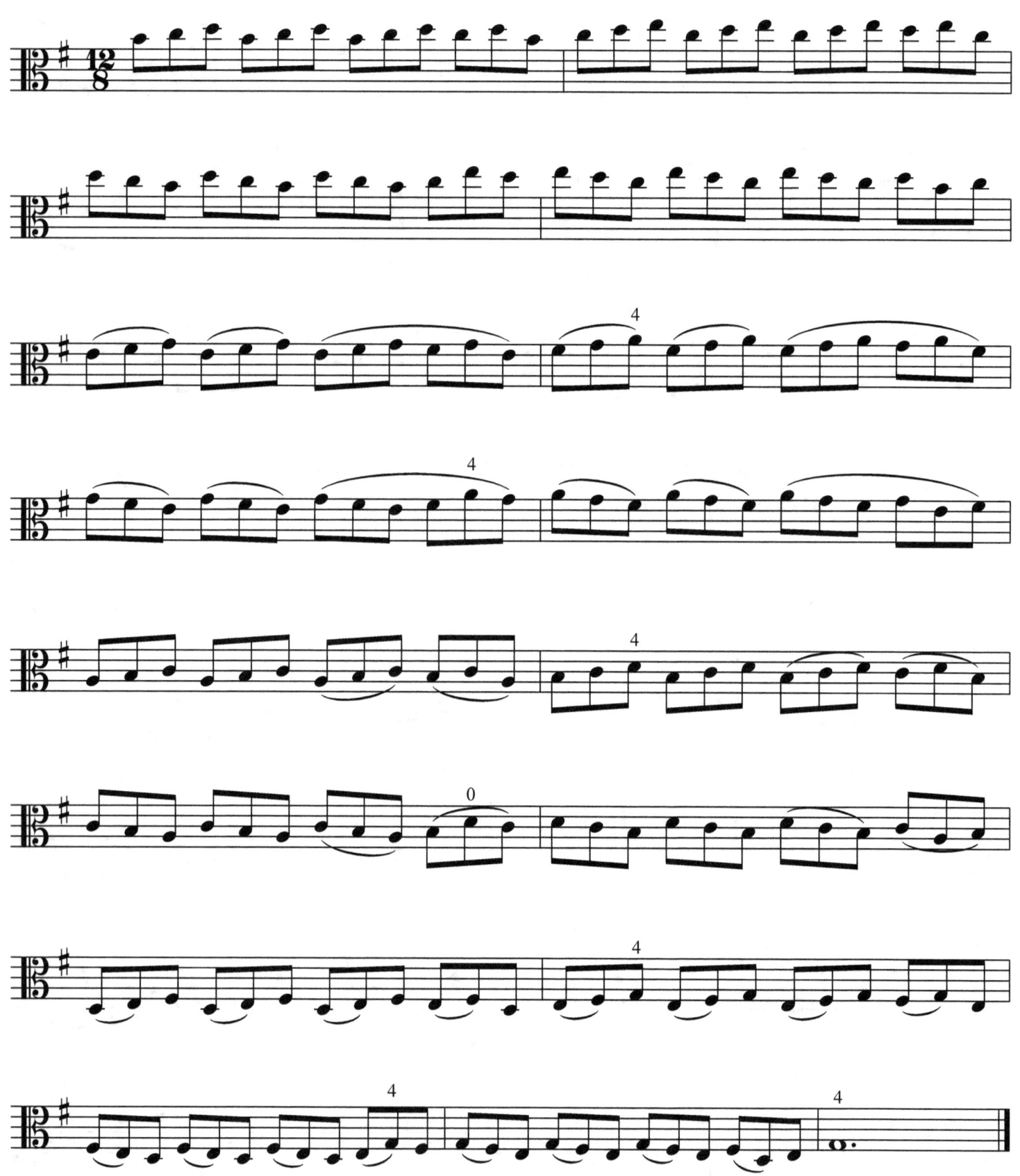

6

John James — Trad., arr. Harvey

Wicklow — Trad., arr. Harvey

©2015 C. Harvey Publications All Rights Reserved.

7

String Crossing

The Triplet Book for Viola, Part One

8

Grenoside Sword Dance Trad., arr. Harvey

The Mischevious Bee Trad., arr. Harvey
(*Andante*)

©2015 C. Harvey Publications All Rights Reserved.

9

Left-Hand Warm-Up

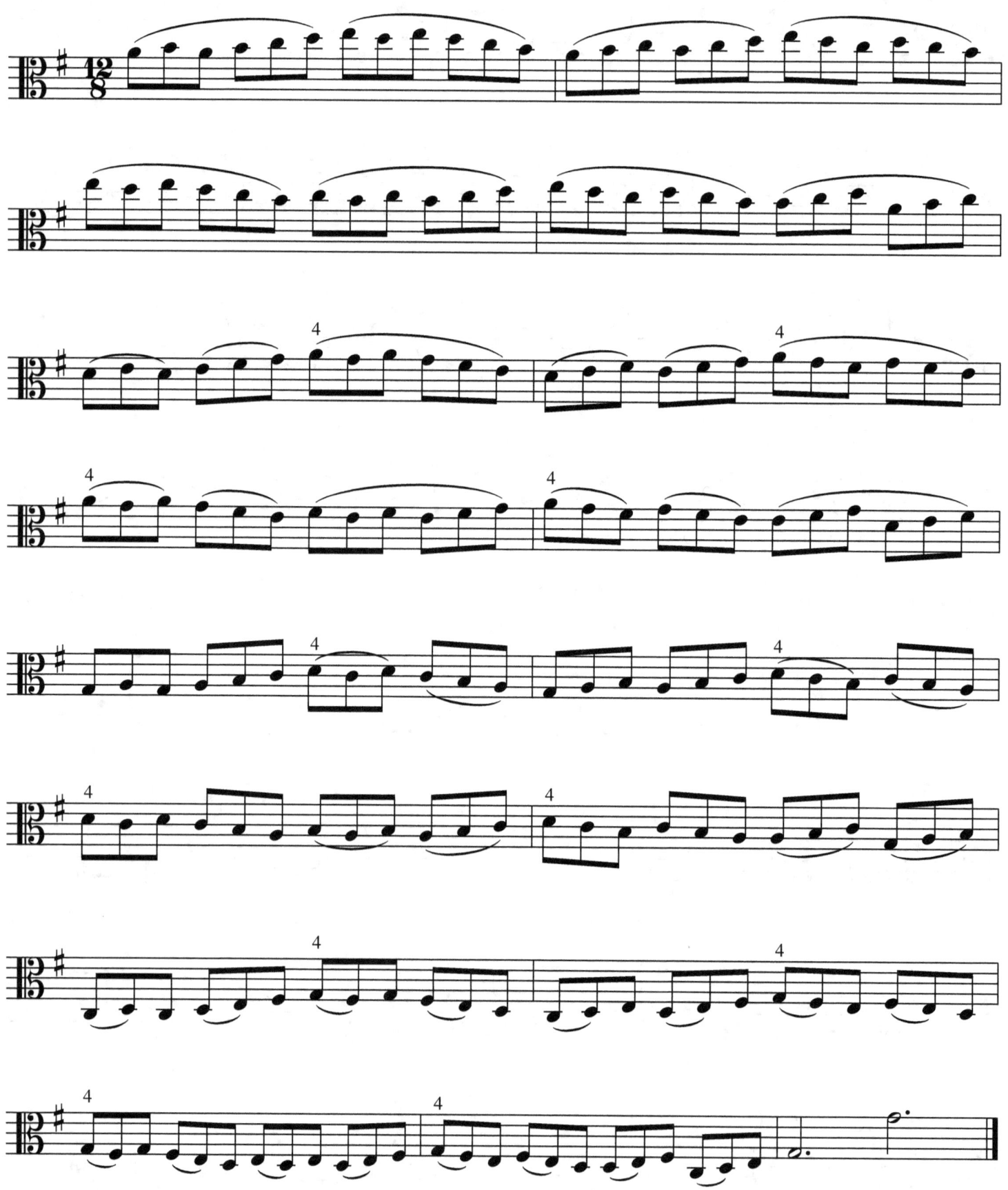

10

Gigue
Bast, arr. Harvey

11

String Crossing

The Triplet Book for Viola, Part One

12

Theme from Concerto Alla Rustica

Vivaldi, arr. Harvey

©2015 C. Harvey Publications All Rights Reserved.

14

Left-Hand Warm-Up: C Major

The Triplet Book for Viola, Part One

13

©2015 C. Harvey Publications All Rights Reserved.

15

String Crossing

16

Even and Odd

Trad., arr. Harvey

17

Left-Hand Warm-Up

18

The Triplet Book for Viola, Part One

The Sprig of Shillelah — Trad., arr. Harvey

Reel — Harvey

19

String Crossing

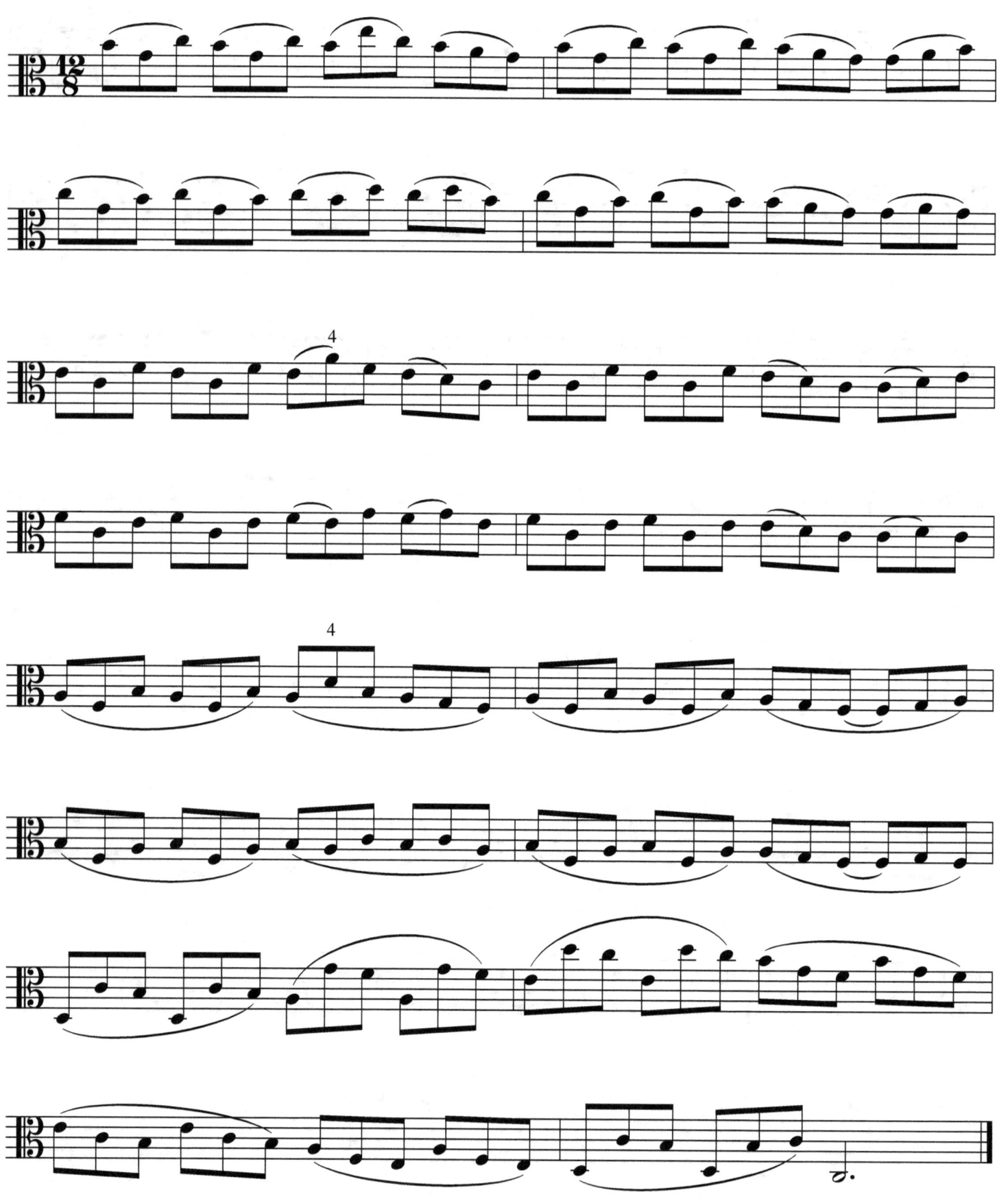

The Triplet Book for Viola, Part One

20

The Drum Major — Trad., arr. Harvey

Oh Dear, What Can the Matter Be — Trad., arr. Harvey

©2015 C. Harvey Publications All Rights Reserved.

21

Left-Hand Warm-Up

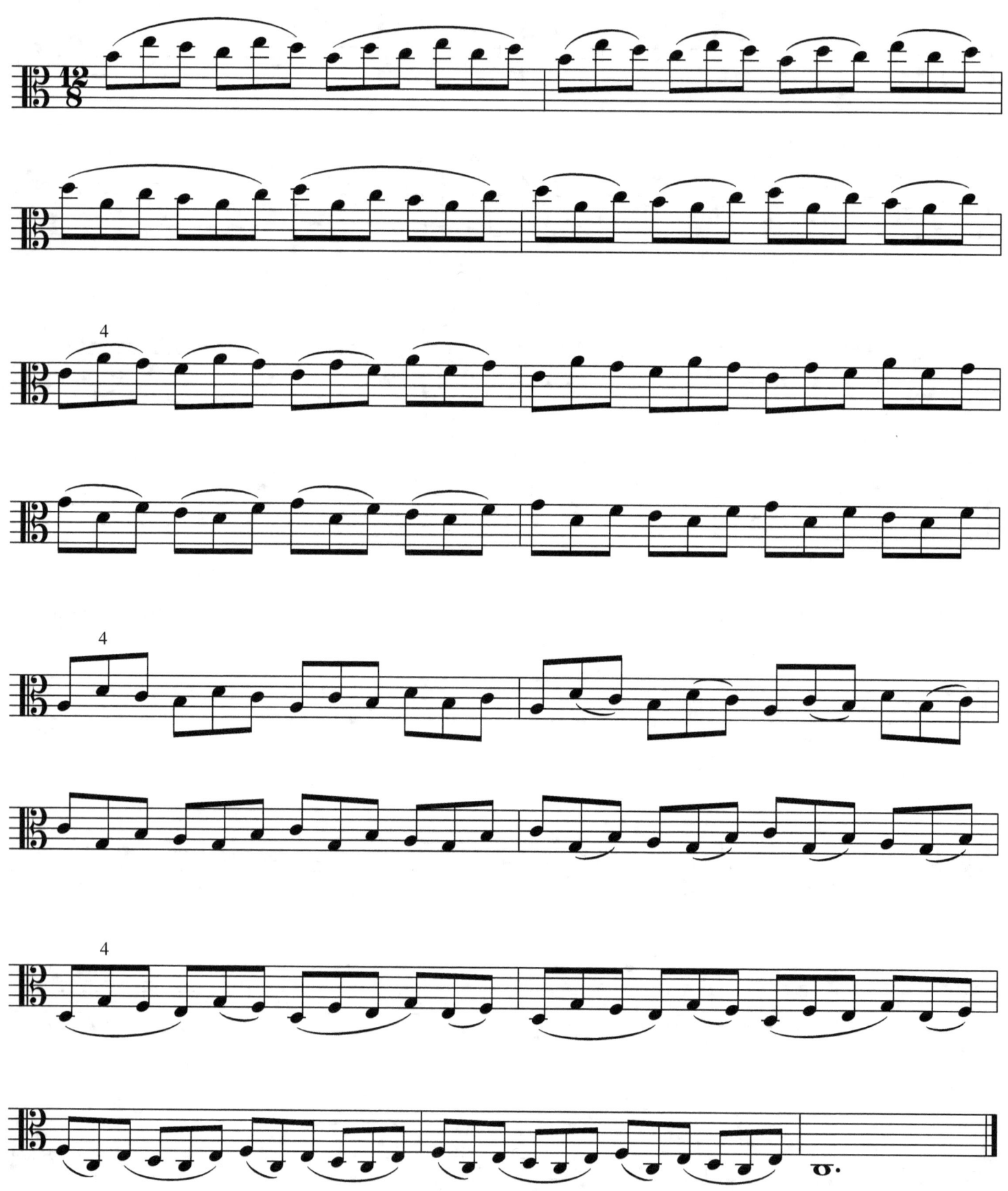

The Triplet Book for Viola, Part One   23

22

La Pastorale   Burgmuller, arr. Harvey

23

String Crossing

The Triplet Book for Viola, Part One
24
Study
Carl Fisher's Method, arr. Harvey

25

Left-Hand Warm-Up: F Major

The Triplet Book for Viola, Part One

©2015 C. Harvey Publications All Rights Reserved.

26

Garry Owen
Trad., arr. Harvey

Gigue
Anon., arr. Harvey

27

String Crossing

The Triplet Book for Viola, Part One

28

The Campbells are Coming Trad., arr. Harvey

Haste to the Wedding! Trad., arr. Harvey

©2015 C. Harvey Publications All Rights Reserved.

29

Left-Hand Warm-Up

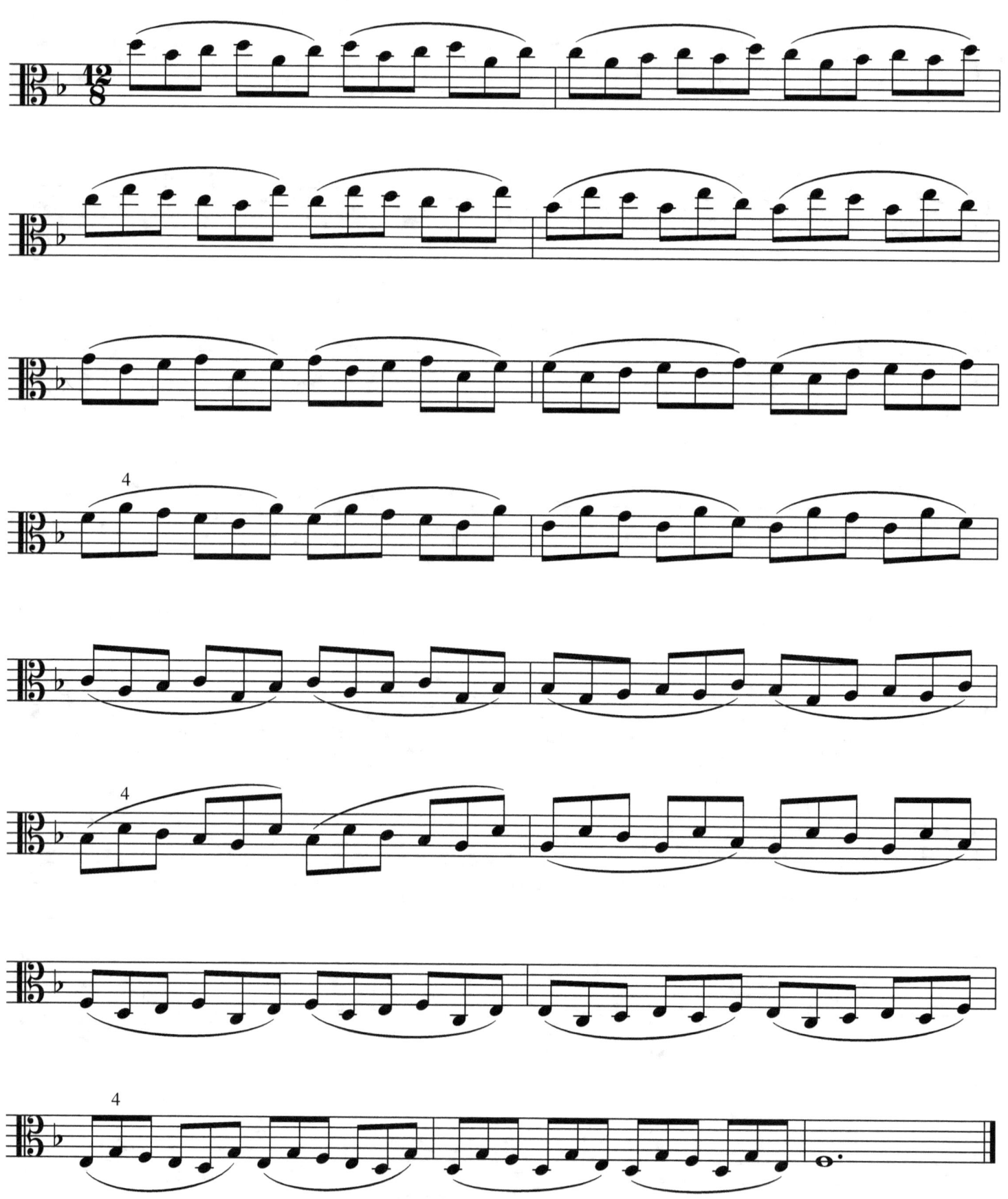

30

The Triplet Book for Viola, Part One

Allegro

Telemann, arr. Harvey

31

String Crossing

The Triplet Book for Viola, Part One

32

Allegro from Brandenburg Concerto No. 6

Bach, arr. Harvey

©2015 C. Harvey Publications All Rights Reserved.

33

Groups of 6

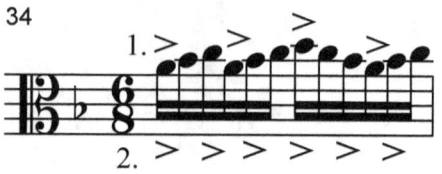

The Triplet Book for Viola, Part One

34

Theme from Brandenburg Concerto No. 3

Bach, arr. Harvey

©2015 C. Harvey Publications All Rights Reserved.

35

Groups of 6

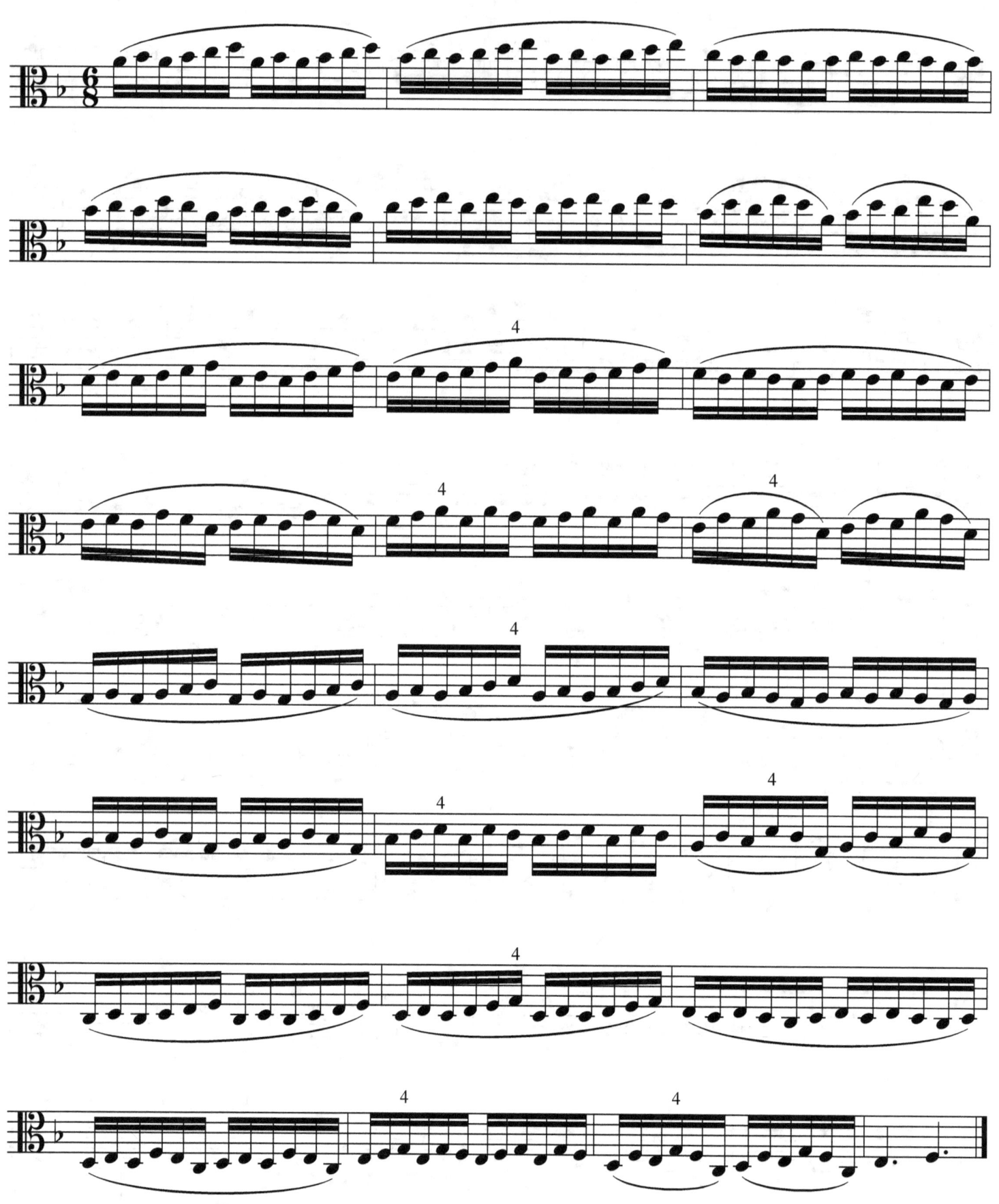

The Triplet Book for Viola, Part One

36

Albinia
Trad., arr. Harvey

©2015 C. Harvey Publications All Rights Reserved.

37

Groups of 6

The Triplet Book for Viola, Part One

38

Lady Cholmolly's Waltz

Trad., arr. Harvey

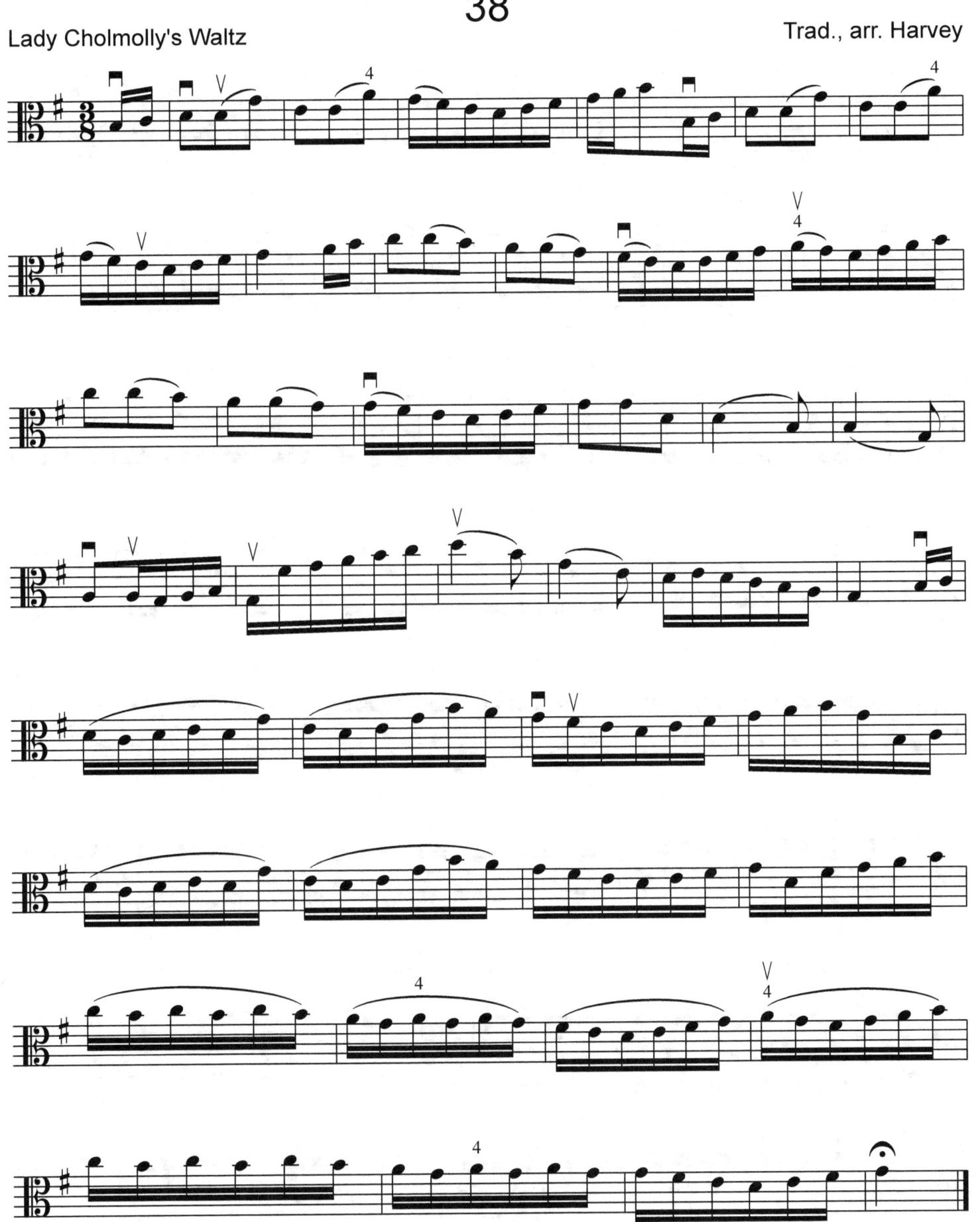

39

Groups of 6

40

Over the Water — Trad., arr. Harvey

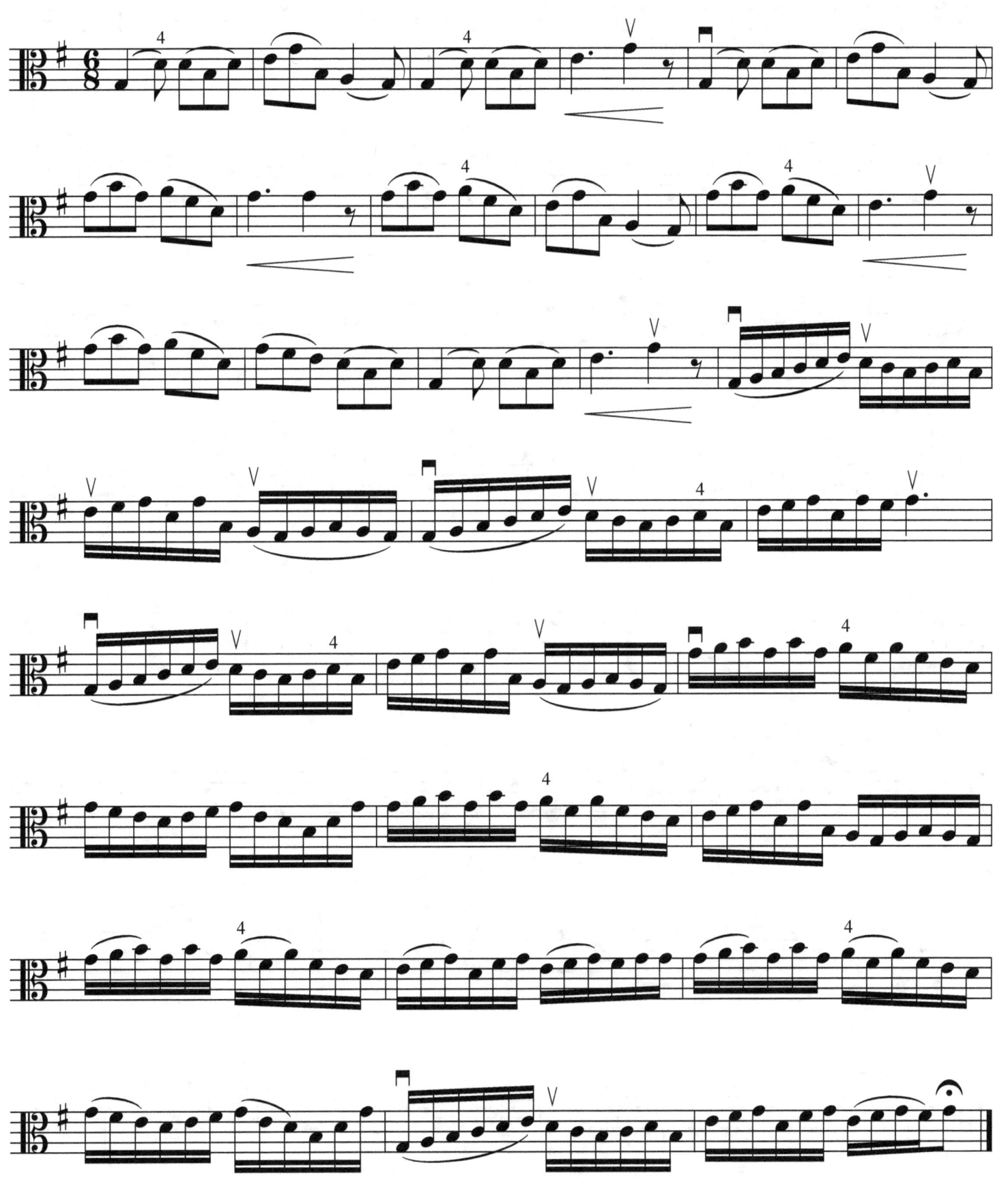

41

Scale Bowings

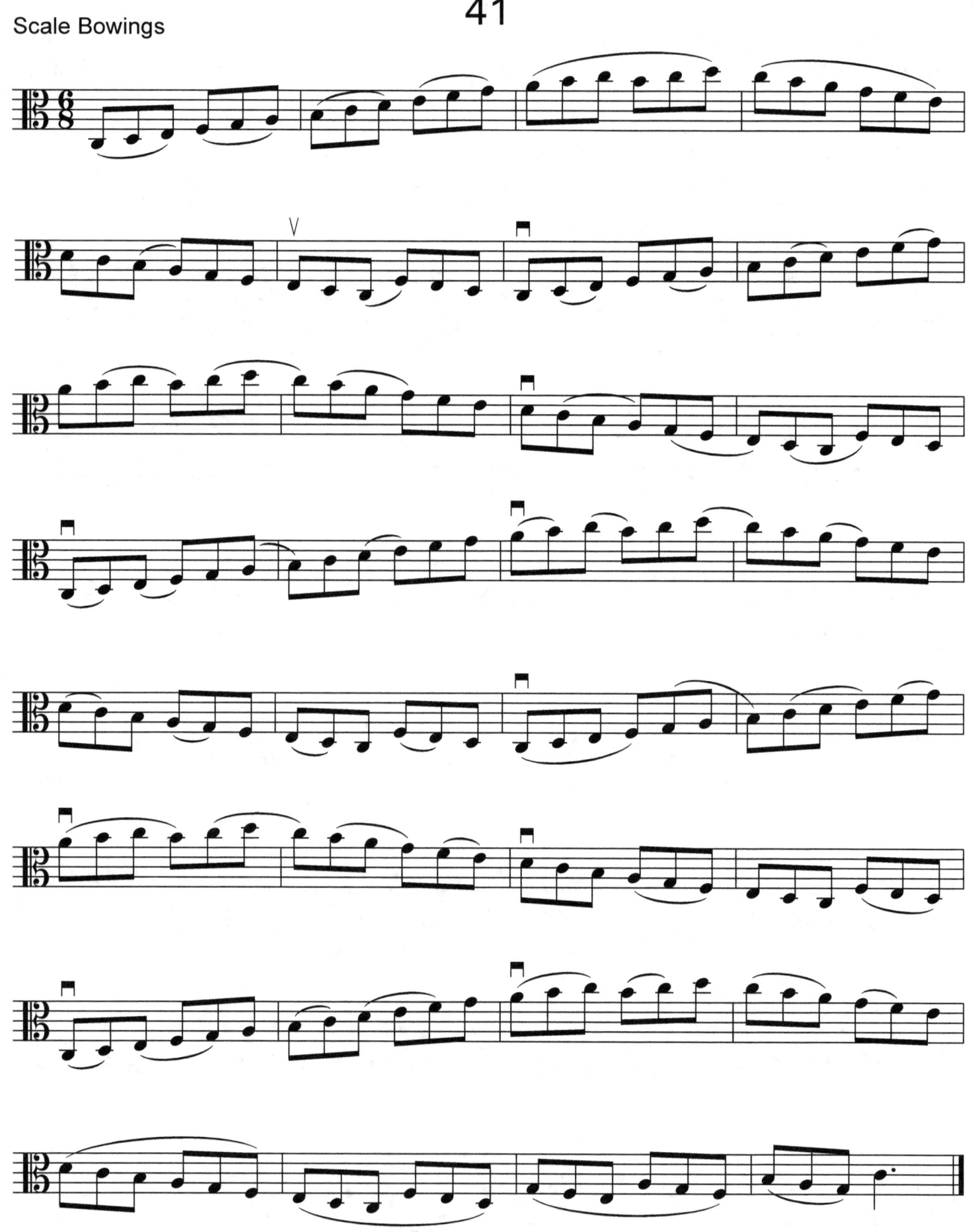

The Triplet Book for Viola, Part One

42

Gigue
Trad., arr. Harvey

©2015 C. Harvey Publications All Rights Reserved.

43

Scale Bowings

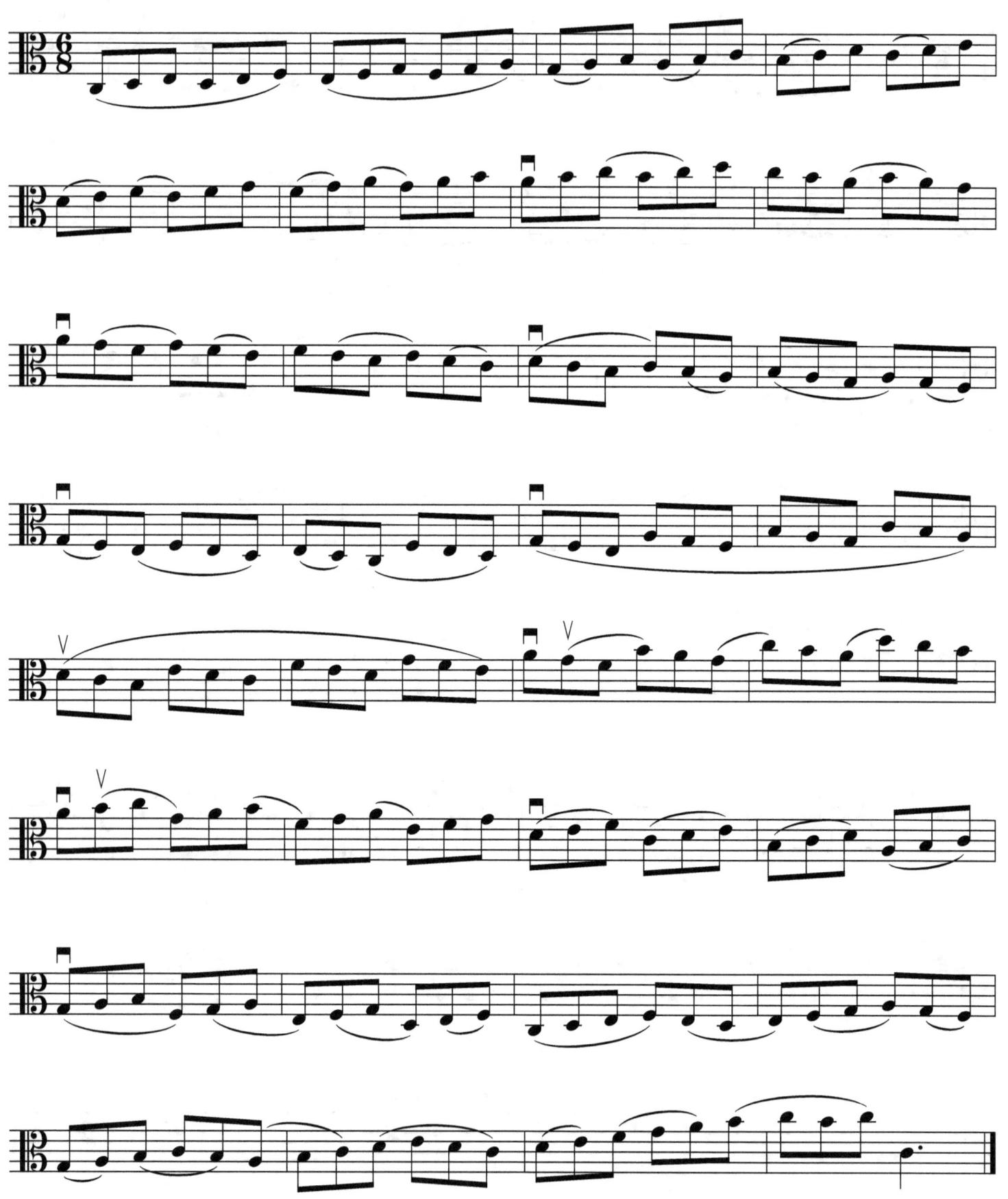

The Triplet Book for Viola, Part One

44

Marabout

Anon., arr. Harvey

©2015 C. Harvey Publications All Rights Reserved.

45

Broken Thirds Bowings

The Triplet Book for Viola, Part One

46

Lord Palmerson's Favourite

Pringle, arr. Harvey

©2015 C. Harvey Publications All Rights Reserved.

47

Arpeggio Bowings

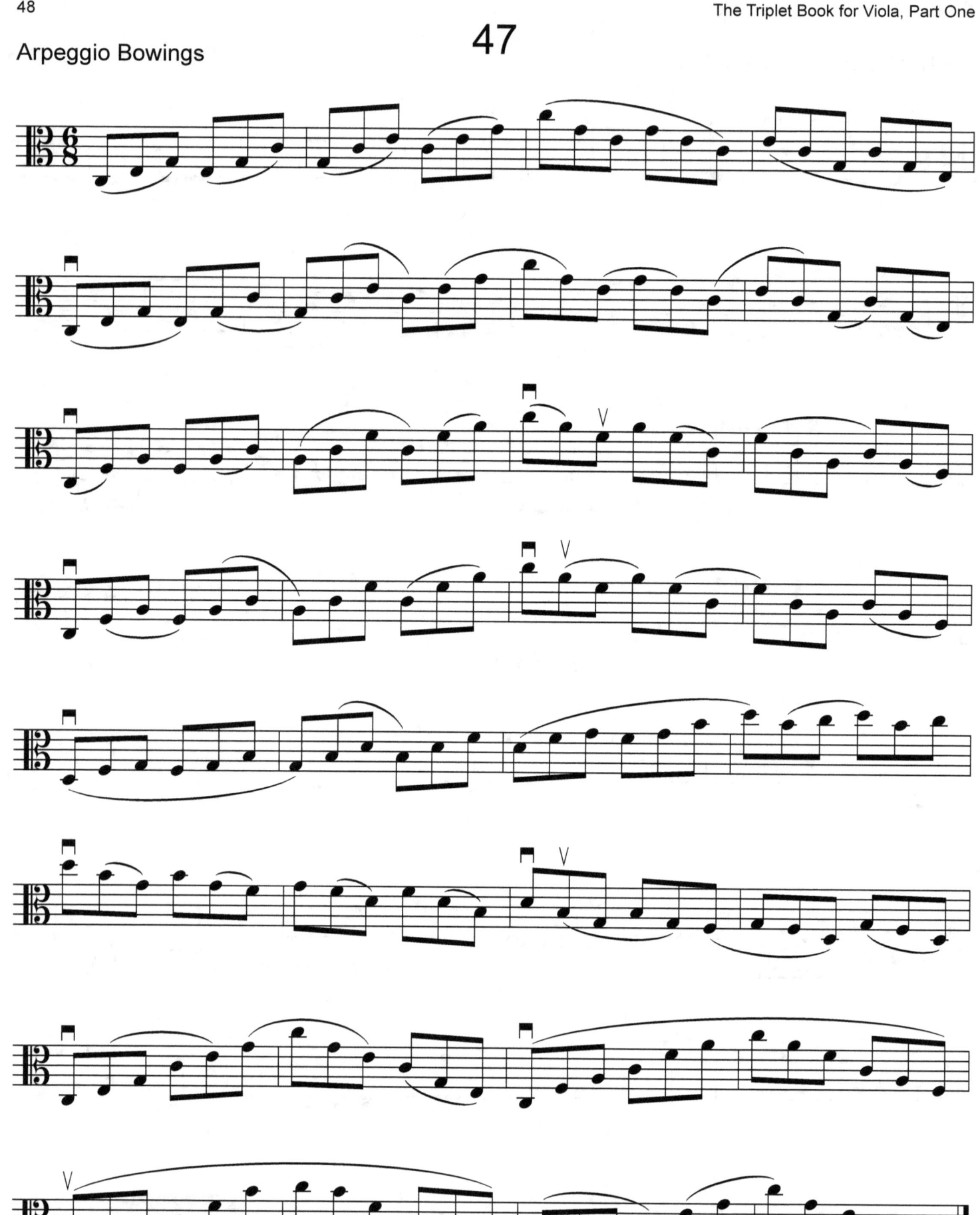

The Triplet Book for Viola, Part One

48

Off She Goes

Trad., arr. Harvey

available from **www.charveypublications.com**: CHP214

Third Position for the Viola, Book One

Cassia Harvey

First Shifting on the D string

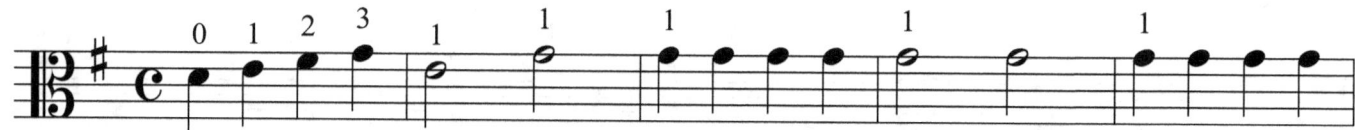

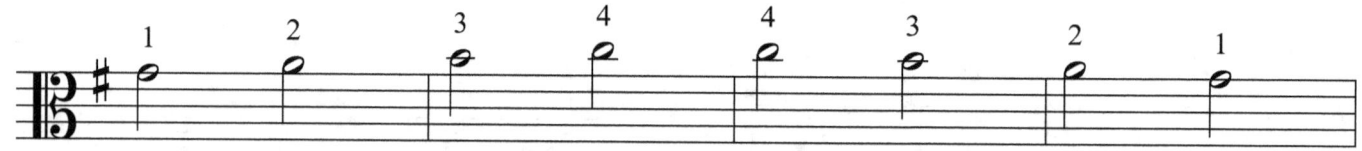

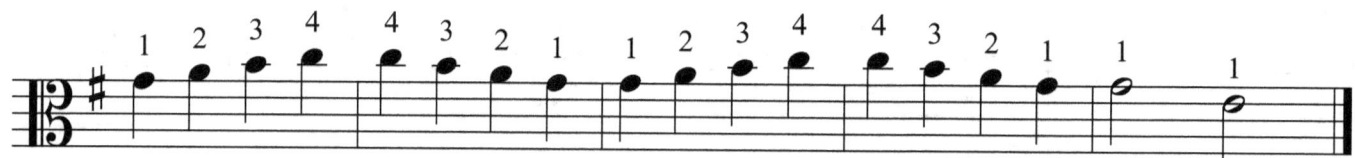

First Shifting on the A string

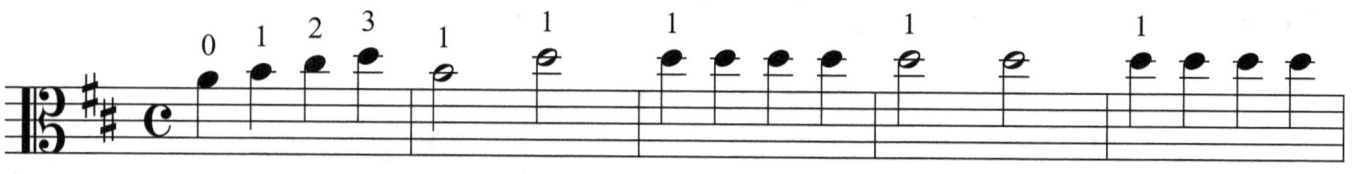

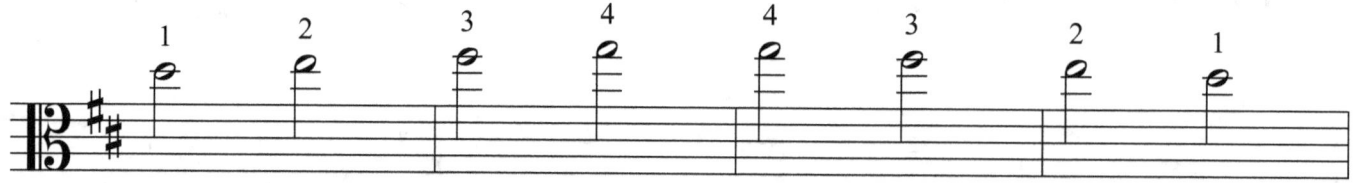

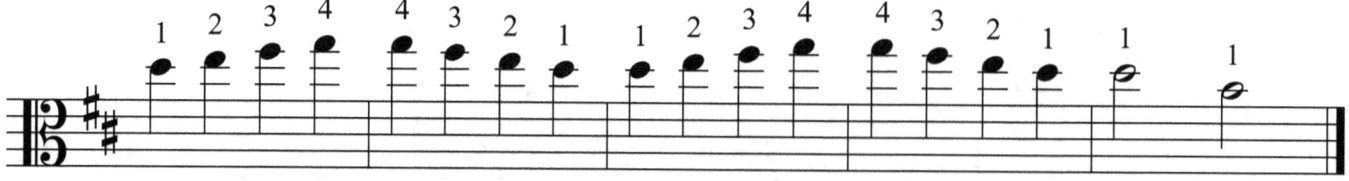

©2012 C. Harvey Publications All Rights Reserved.

www.ingramcontent.com/pod-product-compliance
Lightning Source LLC
Chambersburg PA
CBHW051425070526
44584CB00023B/3585